DEACONS

And

THEIR WIVES

Leo R. LaVinka

Deacons and Their Wives
Copyright © 2021 by Leo R. LaVinka
All Rights Reserved
Printed in the United States of America
May 2021

REL067030: Religion: Christian Theology – Apologetics.

ISBN 978-1-7351454-1-9

All Scripture quotes are from the King James Bible.

No part of this work may be reproduced without the expressed consent of the publisher, except for brief quotes, whether by electronic, photocopying, recording, or information storage and retrieval systems.

Address All Inquiries To:
THE OLD PATHS PUBLICATIONS, Inc.
142 Gold Flume Way
Cleveland, Georgia, U.S.A. 30528

Web: www.theoldpathspublications.com
E-mail: TOP@theoldpathspublications.com

DEDICATION

This book is dedicated to all deacons who have served and who are serving as members of this unique group of God's faithful servants. May God grant that none will let up in his responsibilities as a servant to the people under the authority of his pastor. May all understand and remember their prime purpose and responsibility is to be a SERVANT, to assist in the growth of the church of our Holy God. I also dedicate this book to all men who desire to seek this office. May they prove themselves worthy to be a SERVANT.

Also, I thank my wife and H.D. and Patricia Williams, Directors of The Old Paths Publications for helping to make this book possible.

(Holy God forgive our shortcomings and help us in performing our duties and responsibilities as YOUR servants.)

Leo LaVinka
May 2021

PREFACE

Thank you Brother LaVinka! This is a much-needed book in Bible believing churches today. I have been involved in the ministry for 50 years and have seen far too many churches that have deacons who do not have a clue concerning what their ministry is to be. One church where I was the Director of Christian Education brought men on as deacons because they were successful in business. However, they were far from biblically qualified. In another church, they functioned as a board of directors, trying to give their Pastor instructions as to how I was to do things. One of the men told the Pastor, "I control the money in this church and if you think differently I will do a Mexican Hat Dance on your head!"

When I was called to be Pastor where I have ministered for 42 years, I would not accept the call unless they changed their constitution. Why? Because the Deacon's Chairman was the moderator of the Church. They DID change their constitution and I accepted the call. However, it was an arduous task getting the Deacons to "deac" biblically. Their entire "board mentality" needed to be overhauled and replaced with the biblical role of deacons. It started by me taking charge of the Deacons meetings instead of the "board" chairman.

If only I would have had Brother Leo's book *"Deacons and Their Wives"* back then it would have made the task much easier. He does a Yeoman's job of defining and explaining the work and ministry of Deacons. The book is saturated with Scripture!

I plan on purchasing copies for all my Deacons and plan to make it a part of our devotionals at the beginning of each Deacons meeting. I urge every Pastor, every Deacon, every Deacon's wife and every man who aspires to be a Deacon to get this book and read it.

Pastor David L Brown, Ph.D.
May, 2021

Brother Leo LaVinka has been a very close friend of mine for many years. We have cried together, laughed together, prayed together, and spent time praising the Lord together. My wife, Patricia, and I love his wife and his outstanding family.

Brother Leo has been the "image" of what a biblical deacon should be at our local IFB church. His 50+ years as a church leader, deacon, and many years in the role of head deacon, have always been examples of iron "sharpeneth" iron.

"Iron sharpeneth iron; so a man sharpeneth the countenance of his friend." **Proverbs 27:17**

He is a soul winner beyond a measure. I have witnessed him weep over the lost as he has knocked on doors and attested to his unshakable faith for many years.

The Old Paths Publications (TOP Publications) could not be more pleased that he has chosen our service company to publish this work. We know it will be a blessing to many pastors as they share what a Biblical deacon should be, and to deacons as they learn their true responsibilities before a holy God.

At present, Brother Leo is fighting cancer. His lovely wife, Elsie, is an outstanding deacon's wife. They are going through the "fire," so to speak, but they are both unwavering in their trust in God.

H. D. Williams, M.D., Ph.D.,
President of the "The Old Paths Publications."
May, 2021

FORWARD

The experiences I've had by serving as a deacon for the past fifty plus years in both large and small churches has led me to the conclusion that deacons need to be reminded of what God teaches in His Holy Word concerning their qualifications, selection, and responsibilities. Using the office of a deacon supported by his wife will assist the pastor in growing God's church. Not for the sake of numbers but for the saving of souls and grounding new converts in the Word of God. Deacons are SERVANTS and should SERVE. I'm very much aware that we all sin and fall short of the glory of God. That is especially applicable to me. But none of us have any excuse not to strive for perfection.

> ***Ephesians 2:10*** *For we are his workmanship, created in Christ Jesus unto good works, which God hath before ordained that we should walk in them.*
>
> ***Romans 12:1*** *I beseech you therefore brethren, by the mercies of God, that you present your bodies a living sacrifice, holy, acceptable unto God, which is your reasonable service.*
>
> Leo LaVinka

TABLE OF CONTENTS

DEDICATION 3
FORWARD 7
TABLE OF CONTENTS 8
INTRODUCTION.. 10
    DEACON DEFINED 11
    FINAL WORD 12
    THE BEGINNING 13
    JESUS' INSTRUCTIONS 15
    POWER FROM GOD..17
    THE UNBROKEN CHAIN 18
    WHO CHANGED? 20
    THE WORK OF THE MINISTRY 21
    SOUL WINNING 22
    SEVEN CHOSEN 25
    DEACONS ARE SERVANTS 28
    DEACONS WORK 28
    PROVEN FIRST..29
    WHAT DEACONS ARE AND ARE NOT 31
    PASTORS RESPONSIBILITY TO DEACONS.....................32
    QUALIFICATIONS OF A DEACON 33
    STEPS IN CHOOSING DEACONS 36
    PASTOR'S CHOICE..37
    QUESTIONING DEACONS 37
    DEACONS WIVES 41
    CHURCH APPROVAL...47
    FINDING NEW CANDIDATES 48
    UNDERSTANDING 49
    PASTORS NEEDS...50
    TRUST 51
    DEACONS OFFICES 52
    ROTATION..53
    HIGH WATER MARK 53
    DEACON STEPHEN...54
    DEACON PHILIP 56
    INSPIRATION...57
    FOLLOW THE LEADER 58
    OTHER DUTIES 59
    NEGLECTED DUTIES 60

DEACONS AND THEIR WIVES

DEMONSTRATE FAITH 62
PASTOR/DEACONS MEETINGS 63
STAND 65
CONCLUSION 67
SALVATION 68
INDEX 72
SCRIPTURE REFERENCES 76
ABOUT THE AUTHOR 83

INTRODUCTION

My experience and limited Bible knowledge has demonstrated to me that deacons are sometimes not chosen wisely and many do not understand what the Bible requires from those holding this office. This book is written for the purpose of assisting pastors, deacons, their wives, and those desiring the position as deacon in their understanding of Bible requirements and responsibilities, and how to use this office well. I believe many churches will not grow because pastors are expected to perform many tasks which are clearly the responsibility of all church members, especially deacons. Pastors become overwhelmed in the workload required to pastor and run the many other tasks which others should be performing. One should keep in mind that deacons are not perfect but our goal should be to continue to grow and serve in order to seek perfection.

DEACON DEFINED

The word deacon as defined in "Strong's Concordance" means attendant, host, friend, teacher, minister, to serve, run errands, waiter, or other <u>menial</u> duties. In other words it means SERVANT. They are servants of the people under the direct authority of the pastor. They assist him in <u>any</u> and <u>all</u> ways in which he desires for the purpose of building the body of Christ, the church. It is an honor to <u>serve</u> God as one of His servants.

> ***Matthew 6:24*** *No man can serve two masters: for either he will hate the one, and love the other; or else he will hold to the one, and despise the other. Ye cannot serve God and mammon.*
>
> ***Luke 4:8*** *And Jesus answered and said unto him, Get thee behind me, Satan: for it is written, Thou shalt worship the Lord thy God, and him only shalt thou serve.*
>
> ***John 12:26*** *If any man serve me, let him follow me; and where I am, there shall also my servant be: if any man serve me, him will my Father honour.*
>
> ***Hebrews 9:14*** *How much more shall the blood of Christ, who through the eternal Spirit offered himself without spot to God, purge your conscience from dead works to serve the living God?*

FINAL WORD

The Bible (KJV) is clear on what deacons are and what they are not. What I present here is what I've learned from the Bible and in serving as a deacon for the past fifty plus years under several great pastors such as Curtis Hutson, William Pennell, Don Richards, and others. They used the office of deacons in accordance with God's Holy Word. I need to pause here to say that <u>all</u> Christians are commanded to do the work of the ministry, especially deacons having been <u>proved</u>. For example, Paul addresses the Book of Philippians to <u>all</u> <u>saints</u> with the <u>bishops</u> and <u>deacons</u>.

> ***Philippians 1:1*** *Paul and Timotheus, the servants of Jesus Christ, to all the saints in Christ Jesus which are at Philippi, with the bishops and deacons:*
>
> ***Luke 9:23*** *And he said to them all, If any man will come after me, let him deny himself, and take up his cross daily, and follow me.*

What follows in this book are requirements which I believe God expects from all deacons. Do I believe that as deacons we perform all these responsibilities to the very best of our abilities? The answer is NO! But if we are not striving to do them, and if we are not attempting to improve, then we are failures. It would be hard to find another Philip or Stephen just like it would be hard to find another Peter, John, or Paul. As Curtis

Hutson used to say "Shoot for the moon, you may not hit it, but if you don't try you will never get off the ground." Keep in mind that God would not have given us these responsibilities if he didn't expect us to do them. God will help if we try.

> ***Ephesians 4:12-15*** *For the perfecting of the saints, for the work of the ministry, for the edifying of the body of Christ: Till we all come in the unity of the faith, and of the knowledge of the Son of God, unto a perfect man, unto the measure of the stature of the fulness of Christ: That we henceforth be no more children, tossed to and fro, and carried about with every wind of doctrine, by the sleight of men, and cunning craftiness, whereby they lie in wait to deceive; But speaking the truth in love, may grow up into him in all things, which is the head, even Christ:*

THE BEGINNING

The position of deacons had its beginning in the Day of Pentecost with the start of the New Testament Church. The disciples were filled with the Holy Ghost and multitudes came together and many were saved. First three thousand, then five thousand. Then they taught and preached in every house in Jerusalem. These disciples were soul winners. They were not ashamed of the Gospel of Jesus Christ. As the church grew so did the needs of the people and the church. The apostles could no longer do everything. They needed help. The needs of the people began to be neglected. They started to murmur. The apostles solved that problem with DEACONS. The apostles also began to ordain pastors to serve in ministering to local bodies of believers. It followed that they too would need deacons to assist in the work.

> **Acts 2:41** *Then they that gladly received his word were baptized: and the same day there were added unto them about three thousand souls.*
>
> **Acts 4:4** *Howbeit many of them which heard the word believed; and the number of the men was about five thousand.*
>
> **Acts 5:42** *And daily in the temple, and in every house, they ceased not to teach and preach Jesus Christ.*
>
> **Hebrews 6:9-10** *But, beloved, we are persuaded better things of you, and things that accompany salvation, though we thus speak. For God is not unrighteous to forget your work and labour of love, which ye have shewed toward his name, in that ye have ministered to the saints, and do minister.*

JESUS' INSTRUCTIONS

Drop back in time between the resurrection of Jesus and his ascension into heaven. After Jesus had risen from the tomb he continued to teach his disciples. The things he taught must have been of the utmost importance. He commanded them to go and teach all nations all his commandments. To get them saved, baptized, and grounded in the faith so that they would continue to do the same for others. The purpose was to start an unending unbroken chain in building his church.

> ***Matthew 28:18-20*** *And Jesus came and spake unto them, saying, All power is given unto me in heaven and in earth. Go ye therefore, and teach all nations, baptizing them in the name of the Father, and of the Son, and of the Holy Ghost: Teaching them to observe all things whatsoever I have commanded you: and, lo, I am with you alway, even unto the end of the world. Amen.*

> ***Luke 10:2*** *Therefore said he unto them, The harvest truly is great, but the labourers are few: pray ye therefore the Lord of the harvest, that he would send forth labourers into his harvest.*

Jesus said Go into all the world and preach the gospel to every creature. I often wondered why Jesus used the word creature. I believe he knew

DEACONS AND THEIR WIVES

that if he didn't we would be culling out many groups of lost people who <u>we</u> would judge unworthy. In Luke Jesus in the parable of the man making a feast said "Call the poor, the maimed and the blind." "Go into the highways, the hedges, and <u>compel</u> them to come in, that my house may be filled." The apostles went and in turn you and I became part of this unending and unbroken chain. We should <u>observe</u> this <u>commandment</u> as well as <u>all</u> others. Pastors teach, deacons help, and WE ALL GO!

> ***1 Timothy 3:10*** *And let these also first be proved; then let them use the office of a deacon, being found blameless.* ***1 Timothy 3:13*** *For they that have used the office of a deacon well purchase to themselves a good degree, and great boldness in the faith which is in Christ Jesus.*
>
> ***Mark 16:15*** *And he said unto them, Go ye into all the world, and preach the gospel to every creature.*
>
> ***1 John 2:6*** *He that saith he abideth in him ought himself also so to walk, even as he walked.*
>
> ***1 John 1:6*** *If we say that we have fellowship with him, and walk in darkness, we lie, and do not the truth:*

POWER FROM GOD

The last commandment Jesus told his disciples was not to depart from Jerusalem until they received power after receiving the Holy Ghost to <u>witness</u> to the whole earth. Power to do what? <u>Witness</u>! A person filled with the Holy Ghost <u>will be</u> a witness. There are no exceptions. One of the qualifications for deacons is that they be filled with the Holy Ghost – TO WITNESS.

Paul said he was a debtor to preach to all people. We are also debtors. We have been bought and redeemed with the precious Blood of Jesus Christ. Lost people have a God given right to hear a clear salvation message from all of us who are saved, especially deacons.

> ***Ephesians 1:19*** *And what is the exceeding greatness of his power to us-ward who believe, according to the working of his mighty power,*
>
> ***Acts 1:4-5*** *And, being assembled together with them, commanded them that they should not depart from Jerusalem, but wait for the promise of the Father, which, saith he, ye have heard of me. For John truly baptized with water; but ye shall be baptized with the Holy Ghost not many days hence.*
>
> ***Acts 1:8-9*** *But ye shall receive power, after that the Holy Ghost is come upon*

you: and ye shall be witnesses unto me both in Jerusalem, and in all Judaea, and in Samaria, and unto the uttermost part of the earth. And when he had spoken these things, while they beheld, he was taken up; and a cloud received him out of their sight.

Acts 2:4 *And they were all filled with the Holy Ghost, and began to speak with other tongues, as the Spirit gave them utterance.* **Acts 2:11** *Cretes and Arabians, we do hear them speak in our tongues the wonderful works of God.*

Romans 1:14 *I am debtor both to the Greeks, and to the Barbarians; both to the wise, and to the unwise.*

Philippians 1:27 *Only let your conversation be as it becometh the gospel of Christ: that whether I come and see you, or else be absent, I may hear of your affairs, that ye stand fast in one spirit, with one mind striving together for the faith of the gospel;*

THE UNBROKEN CHAIN

As Jesus had promised at Pentecost, they all received the Holy Ghost and began to witness. I wonder how Jesus feels when He did so much for us and we do so little for Him? Are we as members of God's church really a part of the unending and unbroken chain that God established to build his church? I stand guilty of my own short comings in fulfilling this commandment. I confess I am a very weak length.

> **Luke 9:23** *And he said to them all, If any man will come after me, let him deny himself, and take up his cross daily, and follow me.*
>
> **1 Timothy 1:15** *This is a faithful saying, and worthy of all acceptation, that Christ Jesus came into the world to save sinners; of whom I am chief.*
>
> **Luke 24:45-47** *Then opened he their understanding, that they might understand the scriptures, And said unto them, Thus it is written, and thus it behoved Christ to suffer, and to rise from the dead the third day: And that repentance and remission of sins should be preached in his name among all nations, beginning at Jerusalem.*
>
> **Romans 2:5-6** *But after thy hardness and impenitent heart treasurest up unto thyself wrath against the day of wrath and revelation of the righteous judgment of God; Who will render to every man according to his deeds:*
>
> **Proverbs 1:7** *The fear of the LORD is the beginning of knowledge: but fools despise wisdom and instruction.*

WHO CHANGED?

Jesus' desire and command has not changed from the Day of Pentecost. We have! We make all kinds of excuses as to why we can't serve God like he commands. We have grown complacent in absorbing God's word taught and preached by our pastors and teachers. Some of us are far from being a doer of His word.. We are hearers only. For example, I have heard some say they used to go door to door soul winning, but quit because they could not see any results. Our <u>command</u> is to be <u>prepared</u> and to <u>go</u>. We cannot save anyone. The Holy Spirit must convict, people must repent, and Jesus saves. Many times people only need a friendly voice, encouragement, and/or prayer. I personally believe these types of visits are like giving them a cup of cold water. If so, we will not lose our reward. There is no greater feeling than to be able to help someone, be they family, friends or strangers. To be able to lead them to Christ is joy unspeakable.

> **Acts 4:10-12** *Be it known unto you all, and to all the people of Israel, that by the name of Jesus Christ of Nazareth, whom ye crucified, whom God raised from the dead, even by him doth this man stand here before you whole. This is the stone which was set at nought of you builders, which is become the head of the corner. Neither is there salvation in any other: for there is none other*

name under heaven given among men, whereby we must be saved.

Ephesians 2:10 *For we are his workmanship, created in Christ Jesus unto good works, which God hath before ordained that we should walk in them.*

James 1:22 *But be ye doers of the word, and not hearers only, deceiving your own selves.*

Mark 9:41 *For whosoever shall give you a cup of water to drink in my name, because ye belong to Christ, verily I say unto you, he shall not lose his reward.*

THE WORK OF THE MINISTRY

The prime purpose of Jesus coming to this earth was to save sinners, and the prime purpose of pastors is to perfect his members (the saints) for the work of the ministry. It follows that the prime purpose of deacons is to assist the pastor in accomplishing his charge. Deacons should set an example in serving God's church. Jesus is the cornerstone on which we all build.

Ephesians 4:30 *And grieve not the holy Spirit of God, whereby ye are sealed unto the day of redemption.*

Ephesians 4:11-13 *And he gave some, apostles; and some, prophets;*

and some, evangelists; and some, pastors and teachers; For the perfecting of the saints, for the work of the ministry, for the edifying of the body of Christ: Till we all come in the unity of the faith, and of the knowledge of the Son of God, unto a perfect man, unto the measure of the stature of the fulness of Christ:

James 2:20 *But wilt thou know, O vain man, that faith without works is dead?*

SOUL WINNING

Deacons should set an example for others as a servant to the pastor, but especially to God. They should be soul winners. The Bible has a lot to say about winning souls. For example, in the Book of John, Chapter 25, Jesus said God was the husbandman, He was the vine, and Christians are the branches. He said branches produce fruit. If the fruit of an apple tree is an apple and the fruit of a fig tree is a fig, it follows that the fruit of a Christian is a Christian. Jesus said abide in me and you will bring forth much fruit. Abide here means to stand with Jesus. Be as one with Him. Be steadfast. Don't give up. Much fruit means not a little but a lot. God is our husbandman, Jesus is the vine and if we are attached to them how can we possibly fail? We should be super fruit producers. Jesus invested in us with his precious blood. What do we invest in him? Christians are the salt of the earth, the light of the world. Jesus said, "Let your light shine before men, that they may see your good works and glorify your Father which is in heaven." No fruit means not attached. Dead branches are good for nothing but to be burned like firewood. <u>Saved</u> people can never be lost but they can be unprofitable servants. Oliver Green in his book of John, Volume III, page 21 said, "It is a sad thing indeed when a believer speaks great swelling words and gives great testimony, but offers no fruit --------.". Jesus came to this earth to save sinners. Why do you think he leaves Christians here? Remember Jesus said "Herein is my Father glorified that you bear much fruit so shall ye be my disciples". This is what God expects of ALL Christians. What do you think he expects of deacons?

> ***1 Corinthians 3:7-8*** *So then neither is he that planteth any thing, neither he that watereth; but God that giveth the increase. Now he that planteth and he that watereth are one: and every man shall receive his own reward according to his own labour.*
>
> ***John 15:1-8*** *I am the true vine, and my Father is the husbandman. Every branch in me that beareth not fruit he taketh away: and every branch that beareth fruit, he purgeth it, that it may bring forth more fruit. Now ye are clean through the word which I have spoken unto you. Abide in me, and I in you. As the branch cannot bear fruit of itself,*

except it abide in the vine; no more can ye, except ye abide in me. I am the vine, ye are the branches: He that abideth in me, and I in him, the same bringeth forth much fruit: for without me ye can do nothing. If a man abide not in me, he is cast forth as a branch, and is withered; and men gather them, and cast them into the fire, and they are burned. If ye abide in me, and my words abide in you, ye shall ask what ye will, and it shall be done unto you. Herein is my Father glorified, that ye bear much fruit; so shall ye be my disciples.

John 15:16 *Ye have not chosen me, but I have chosen you, and ordained you, that ye should go and bring forth fruit, and that your fruit should remain: that whatsoever ye shall ask of the Father in my name, he may give it you.*

Matthew 5:13-16 *Ye are the salt of the earth: but if the salt have lost his savour, wherewith shall it be salted? it is thenceforth good for nothing, but to be cast out, and to be trodden under foot of men. Ye are the light of the world. A city that is set on an hill cannot be hid. Neither do men light a candle, and put it under a bushel, but on a candlestick; and it giveth light unto all that are in the house. Let your light so* *shine before men, that they may see your good works, and glorify your Father which is in heaven.*

SEVEN CHOSEN

As the New Testament Church grew so did the need for servants. At first only seven were needed. The apostles were overworked to the point it hindered their ability to pray and minister as they knew they should. They instructed the brethren to find seven men of honest report, full of the Holy Ghost and wisdom to be over these neglected tasks. They did and the disciples multiplied and the church grew. These men were a part of the Pentecost revival and had <u>already</u> proved themselves to be honest, full of the Holy Ghost and wisdom. They were <u>not</u> chosen at random or for their popularity. They were <u>proven</u> servants. This selection procedure "pleased the <u>whole</u> multitude". They all had input in the selection. These men were selected to serve tables <u>and</u> <u>most</u> importantly to relieve the apostles of menial tasks which hindered their ministry. It is obvious that the terms "widows were neglected in the daily ministration" and "serving tables" are not to be construed as written in stone as their one and only duty. The main purpose was to perform everything necessary to assure support to the people and <u>especially</u> to relieve the ministers of tasks which would hinder their work. These men were to be ordained as SERVANTS. As the churches grew, so did the task to be performed in order to grow the church. I have heard good men say that the only requirement for deacons in the Bible is to help the widows and serve tables. Nothing could be further from the truth. All Christians, but especially proven deacons, are to keep all God's commandments, precepts, and His entire Words.

> **Revelation 14:12** *Here is the patience of the saints: here are they that keep the commandments of God, and the faith of Jesus.*
>
> **1 John 2:4** *He that saith, I know him, and keepeth not his commandments, is a liar, and the truth is not in him.*
>
> **Romans 10:17** *So then faith cometh by hearing, and hearing by the word of God.*
>
> **John 5:24** *Verily, verily, I say unto you, He that heareth my word, and believeth on him that sent me, hath everlasting life, and shall not come into condemnation; but is passed from death unto life.*
>
> **John 8:31** *Then said Jesus to those Jews which believed on him, If ye continue in my word, then are ye my disciples indeed;*
>
> **1 John 5:10** *He that believeth on the Son of God hath the witness in himself: he that believeth not God hath made*

him a liar; because he believeth not the record that God gave of his Son.

Acts 6:1-7 *And in those days, when the number of the disciples was multiplied, there arose a murmuring of the Grecians against the Hebrews, because their widows were neglected in the daily ministration. Then the twelve called the multitude of the disciples unto them, and said, It is not reason that we should leave the word of God, and serve tables. Wherefore, brethren, look ye out among you seven men of honest report, full of the Holy Ghost and wisdom, whom we may appoint over this business. We will give ourselves continually to prayer, and to the ministry of* **the word**. *And the saying pleased the whole multitude: and they chose Stephen, a man full of faith and of the Holy Ghost, and Philip, and Prochorus, and Nicanor, and Timon, and Parmenas, and Nicolas a proselyte of Antioch: Whom they set before the apostles: and when they had prayed, they laid their hands on them. And the word of God increased; and the number of the disciples multiplied in Jerusalem greatly; and a great company of the priests were obedient to the faith.*

DEACONS ARE SERVANTS

Deacons were NOT a committee. They were NOT overseers of the church. They were servants. These men, later called deacons, were to be faithful men of the local church who had a proven track record. They were set apart to assist the ministers in preserving their valuable time. They were ONLY ordained when there was a need. They were NOT chosen to be a tin god. They were servants. They were to be "among you", meaning men who were believers and church members. They were to be honest or reputable. They were to be full of the Holy Ghost. That is to be spiritual and soul winners. They had to be wise. That is have the intelligence to perform required duties. They were to be servants appointed to perform church business. "Whom we may appoint over this business" means the church leadership delegates. It follows that leadership must hold these deacons accountable. If they don't menial tasks will return to the ministers and it will hinder church growth. To have a strong church everyone needs to work, especially pastors and deacons.

> **Ephesians 6:10** Finally, my brethren, be strong in the Lord, and in the power of his might.

DEACONS WORK

Today we have pastors and teachers for perfecting the saints for the work of the ministry. That is building the church, the body of believers.

It is impossible to expect a pastor to study, teach, preach, care for his flock, and do all the other tasks required to build his church. That in itself is more than a full time job. **ALL** church members have a responsibility to help, especially deacons. Deacons are appointed over specific tasks which are very important and usually repetitive. Tasks appointed do not require rocket ship brain power. They are menial tasks fit for a SERVANT.

> **Ephesians 4:11-12** *And he gave some, apostles; and some, prophets; and some, evangelists; and some, pastors and teachers; For the perfecting of the saints, for the work of the ministry, for the edifying of the body of Christ:*
>
> **Ephesians 5:1** *Be ye therefore followers of God, as dear children;*

PROVEN FIRST

One may ask how could they prepare and prove themselves in seeking a position as a deacon? The answer is simple, study scriptures, live by them, do God's commandments, look around for things being neglected and do them. Again, not to build rocket ships but to perform menial tasks such as greet visitors, keeping neat pews, fixing church sign, visiting sick, sending out cards, keeping church clean and orderly, teaching a Sunday School class, door knocking, cleaning fellowship hall, serving in a church office such as

DEACONS AND THEIR WIVES

secretary, treasurer, Sunday School Superintendent, ordering Sunday School material, and the list goes on and on and on. Ask the pastor how you can help. Just look, ask, be prepared and do! Many times ladies of the church put the men to shame by their faithfulness in finding and performing many tasks while the men sit idle. Men, are we so lazy that we can't see or do? Are we going to stand boldly at the Judgment Seat, look Jesus in the eye and tell him we were not ready when <u>He was ready for the cross and all it demanded</u>?

> **2 Timothy 2:15** *Study to shew thyself approved unto God, a workman that needeth not to be ashamed, rightly dividing the word of truth.*
>
> **1 Corinthians 15:58** *Therefore, my beloved brethren, be ye stedfast, unmoveable, always abounding in the work of the Lord, forasmuch as ye know that your labour is not in vain in the Lord.*
>
> **Luke 9:26** *For whosoever shall be ashamed of me and of my words, of him shall the Son of man be ashamed, when he shall come in his own glory, and in his Father's, and of the holy angels.*
>
> **Romans 9:23** *And that he might make known the riches of his glory on the*

vessels of mercy, which he had afore prepared unto glory,

WHAT DEACONS ARE AND ARE NOT

Sometimes deacons have acquired power which God never intended them to have. They would assume responsibility and power even over the pastor. For this reason some pastors thought the first thing they should do as a new pastor was to get rid of all their deacons. How sad! Deacons are not rulers of a pastor or a church. They do all their duties at the discretion of the pastor. To feel intimidated is the fault of the pastor for not leading and taking charge, and the fault of deacons for assuming power they have no right to have. This condition must be corrected for a church to succeed. Pastors may seek the advice of a deacon, a deacon board, or anyone else as he desires. Deacons also have a responsibility to look after the needs of the pastor and his family especially by offering encouragement and informing him of any problems of which he was not aware. If a church loses their pastor deacons may be appointed by the church to perform certain duties until a new pastor is called. In such case they report back to the church. Such responsibilities should be detailed in the Church Bylaws. In all cases deacons serve as servants of the church. Pastor's pastor, deacons "deak."

Acts 6:3 *Wherefore, brethren, look ye out among you seven men of honest* *report, full of the Holy Ghost and wisdom, whom we may appoint over this business.*

2 Timothy 2:15 *Study to shew thyself approved unto God, a workman that needeth not to be ashamed, rightly dividing the word of truth.*

Romans 1:16 *For I am not ashamed of the gospel of Christ: for it is the power of God unto salvation to every one that believeth; to the Jew first, and also to the Greek.*

PASTORS RESPONSIBILITY TO DEACONS

Pastors have a responsibility to teach and inform deacons as to what they expect them to accomplish (His vision). He <u>must</u> hold them accountable for appointed duties. Scheduled deacon meetings are necessary and are a great way to have harmony and to establish and teach responsibilities. Meetings also support the church and establish pastoral leadership. Not to have meetings is very discouraging to deacons telling them very clearly that they are not needed and they are deacons in name only. HOW SAD! Keep in mind there are no perfect pastors or deacons. We all are sinners and fall short of the glory of God.

Pastor Bill Penell had regular meetings with his deacons. Not only for regular business but for the purpose of teaching us what deacons are and are not, how deacons are chosen, duties of wives, and many other things. He even established fellowships with his deacons where he and all deacons took turns providing suppers at our homes.

> *Romans 3:10, 23* **Romans 3:10** *As it is written, There is none righteous, no, not one:*
>
> **Romans 3:23** *For all have sinned, and come short of the glory of God;*
>
> **James 2:10** *For whosoever shall keep the whole law, and yet offend in one point, he is guilty of all.*
>
> **Ecclesiastes 7:20** *For there is not a just man upon earth, that doeth good, and sinneth not.*
>
> **Proverbs 29:18** *Where there is no vision, the people perish: but he that keepeth the law, happy is he.*

QUALIFICATIONS OF A DEACON

The Bible teaches that "If a man desires the office of a bishop, he desireth a good work." It goes on to define the qualifications of a bishop (preacher). Paul instructing Timothy says "Likewise must the deacons ……" **Likewise,** means similar, like if a man desires the office of a deacon he desires a good work.

DEACONS AND THEIR WIVES

1 Timothy 3:1-8 *This is a true saying, If a man desire the office of a bishop, he desireth a good work. A bishop then must be blameless, the husband of one wife, vigilant, sober, of good behaviour, given to hospitality, apt to teach; Not given to wine, no striker, not greedy of filthy lucre; but patient, not a brawler, not covetous; One that ruleth well his own house, having his children in subjection with all gravity; (For if a man know not how to rule his own house, how shall he take care of the church of God?) Not a novice, lest being lifted up with pride he fall into the condemnation of the devil. Moreover he must have a good report of them which are without; lest he fall into reproach and the snare of the devil.* **Likewise** *must the deacons be grave, not doubletongued, not given to much wine, not greedy of filthy lucre;*

Qualifications of a deacon are listed starting in I Timothy 3:8. Deacons must be grave or dignified. They are not to be double tongued, deceitful, insecure, a gossiper, or not serious. They are not to be given to much wine meaning not addicted, inclined to abuse it. Drunkards shall not inherit the Kingdom of God. Strong drink should be avoided at all cost.

> ***Proverbs 20:1*** *Wine is a mocker, strong drink is raging: and whosoever is deceived thereby is not wise.*
>
> ***Habakkuk 2:15*** *Woe unto him that giveth his neighbour drink, that puttest thy bottle to him, and makest him drunken also, that thou mayest look on their nakedness!*

Deacons must not be greedy of filthy lucre. That is not taking advantage of people. They must be true to the faith attempting to live by the entire word of God. Last, but very important and often overlooked, is that they must FIRST be proved. Proved means to examine like a trial to determine worthiness. They must have <u>demonstrated</u> by their service that they would be faithful to their duties as a deacon. Let them be found blameless, free of any charge, by performing God's work to the best of their ability. In so doing they will obtain good standing and great <u>boldness</u> in the faith. Boldness implies telling others about Christ with <u>no</u> reservations. They are to be a husband of one wife and rule their children and house well. Lastly, they are to use their responsibility as a deacon **well** with great **boldness**.

Their wives must also "....be grave, not slanderous, sober, faithful in all things." They must be separated unto Jesus Christ and from the world.

> ***1 Timothy 3:8-13*** *Likewise must the deacons be grave, not doubletongued, not given to much wine, not greedy of*

filthy lucre; Holding the mystery of the faith in a pure conscience. And let these also first be proved; then let them use the office of a deacon, being found blameless. Even so must their wives be grave, not slanderers, sober, faithful in all things. Let the deacons be the husbands of one wife, ruling their children and their own houses well. For they that have used the office of a deacon well purchase to themselves a good degree, and great boldness in the faith which is in Christ Jesus.

STEPS IN CHOOSING DEACONS

Consider the Bible steps in choosing deacons.

1. There was a need.
2. The need was recognized by the ministers and the people.
3. It would relieve the apostles to give attention to their duties.
4. Qualified proven men were sought.
5. It appears self-evident they were questioned.
6. They were approved by the church.
7. Approval consisted of the laying on of hands by the ministers.
8. They <u>served</u> and the church grew.

PASTOR'S CHOICE

Pastors must always exercise their authority to approve or disapprove a candidate before any other procedure is taken. He could have a personality conflict or he could be aware of situations which could create problems. After that the pastor, deacons, and other ordained men in the church (and others if necessary) should meet together to discuss proposed candidates before they are questioned. If reasons for rejection are found they should not be considered any further. If no objection is found the next step would be questioning the candidate.

QUESTIONING DEACONS

Choosing a deacon <u>after</u> they have proven themselves should not be taken lightly. Questioning a candidate should be thorough. The pastor and others such as ordained preachers and deacons should do the questioning. Some examples of questions which could be asked a candidate are as follows.

1. Have you read and do you believe and do you agree with the Statement of Faith, Covenant, and Bylaws of this church?
2. Would you be willing to faithfully serve this church as a deacon should you be selected?
3. Tell us of your salvation experience.

DEACONS AND THEIR WIVES

4. Do you believe that our Bible was written by men inspired by God to write down every word to the last jot and tittle and that it is forever settled in heaven?
5. Do you believe that the King James Bible is an accurate word for word translation preserved by God to the English-speaking people and therefore contains No error?
6. Do you believe in a triune God consisting of God the Father, God the Son, and God the Holy Spirit?
7. Do you believe in the virgin birth of Jesus Christ, and that he came to this earth for the purpose of saving sinners?
8. Do you believe Jesus lived and died on this earth as 100% man while maintaining his deity as 100% God?
9. Do you believe all people (other than Jesus) are sinners and as such they are lost on their way to an eternal hell separated forever from God for all eternity, and they must repent and trust Jesus for their salvation?
10. Do you believe that without the shedding of the Blood of Jesus Christ on the cross there is no remission for our sins?
11. Do you believe there is a heaven and New Jerusalem where the redeemed of the church will reside with eternal joy and happiness and for all eternity and so shall they ever be with Jesus Christ?

12. Do you believe in the bodily resurrection of Jesus Christ after spending three days and three nights in the tomb?
13. Do you believe Jesus is coming again for his church, the body of believers?
14. Do you believe the Lord's Supper is required by all believers and is symbolic in remembering Jesus Christ, his broken body, and his shed blood which was necessary to redeem sinners, and that we are to use that opportunity to search ourselves, confess our sins, and be worthy of participating in this event?
15. Do you believe in the eternal security of those who trust and believe in Jesus Christ?
16. Do you believe that if Christians confess their sins they will be forgiven?
17. Do you believe that unconfessed and habitual sins of a saint will bring chastisement?
18. Do you believe there are only two ordinances of the church, baptism and the Lord's Supper?
19. Do you believe baptism is symbolic of the death, burial, and resurrection of Jesus Christ and that it demonstrates to others your faith in Him?
20. Do you believe all church members should support the church with their tithes, offerings, and their time?
21. Do you believe churches are commanded to support missionaries?

22. Do you believe in the pretribulation return of Christ for his church?
23. Do you believe a Spirit filled person is a dedicated witness for Jesus Christ?
24. Do you have daily devotions?
25. Do you rule your house for God to the best of your ability?
26. Have you ever been arrested? If so explain.
27. Do you believe a deacon is only a servant of the people under the leadership of his pastor?
28. Do you believe all Spirit filled Christians are soul winners?
29. Do you habitually pass out Bible tracts?
30. Do you GO soulwinning? Explain.
31. Should you be selected as a deacon are you ready to assist the pastor in the ministries to the very best of your ability?
32. Tell us about your service to God.

Acts 6:3 *Wherefore, brethren, look ye out among you seven men of honest report, full of the Holy Ghost and wisdom, whom we may appoint over this business.*

1 Timothy 3:10 *And let these also first be proved; then let them use the office of a deacon, being found blameless.*

DEACONS WIVES

After the questioning of a deacon is completed, the board should meet to discuss the qualifications of the candidate. If they conclude the candidate is qualified and acceptable the candidate should be notified but it should not yet be made public. A meeting should then be arranged through the candidate for the board to meet with the candidate's wife for questioning her. The candidate should escort his wife to the meeting but he should be asked to leave before the questioning begins.

For deacons to be effective in their responsibilities their wives must be 100% supportive of his and her responsibilities. Otherwise conflicts will surely arise with time spent away from home and their preparation and church responsibilities within the home.

Contrary to popular practice, deacons' wives also have responsibilities clearly detailed in the Bible. For example, a deacon cannot rule his house well without the full support and understanding of his wife while she performs the enormous duties of a housewife! Many have added responsibilities of a job to help support the family. Husbands and wives must always support one another. Paul instructing deacons said, "Even so must their wives be grave, not slanderers, sober, faithful in all things."

> **1 Timothy 3:11** *Even so must their wives be grave, not slanderers, sober, faithful in all things.*

DEACONS AND THEIR WIVES

Paul having instructed Timothy in the qualifications as a bishop. (Greek overseer; English pastor) said, "Likewise referring to deacons. He said first let them be "proved" being found blameless. Referring to their wives he said, "Even so must their wives be grave, not slanderers, sober, faithful in all things." "Even so" has the same meaning as "likewise" in verse 8. "Must" means what is right and necessary. Things performed as a sense of duty. "Grace" means dignified and serious in all things. "Not slanderers" means they should not be a gossiper or false accuser like spreading accusations and rumors in the church or community. Keep in mind how serious this is by remembering that Satan is the accuser of the brethren before God. "Sober" means sober minded, self control, of a sound mind. (Definitions are mostly taken from "An expository Dictionary of Bible Words" by W. E. Vine, Merrill F, Unger, & William White.) "Faithful in all things" means <u>ALL</u> things. That is <u>ALL</u> things! It is most important that if these instructions to Timothy are studied carefully they reveal that wives also must FIRST be proved. They should have already demonstrated their love and devotion to our Lord by their service. In a sense the deacon and his wife serve as a team by supporting one another as a deacon and his wife.

1 Timothy 3:8 *Likewise must the deacons be grave, not doubletongued, not given to much wine, not greedy of filthy lucre;*

Titus 2:3 *The aged women likewise, that they be in behaviour as becometh holiness, not false accusers, not given to much wine, teachers of good things;*

Duties that a wife may perform could include:

1. Teaching children.
2. Nursery duties.
3. Calling sick and absentees.
4. Mailing cards for sick, absentees, birthdays, visitors, etc.
5. Taking charge of fellowships.
6. Ordering literature.
7. Visiting sick and shut ins.
8. Passing out tracts.
9. The numerous tasks required for fellowships.
10. The list goes on and on.

Titus 2:1 *But speak thou the things which become sound doctrine:*

Titus 2:3-5 *The aged women likewise, that they be in behaviour as becometh holiness, not false accusers, not given to much wine, teachers of good things; That they may teach the young women to be sober, to love their husbands, to love their children, To be discreet, chaste, keepers at home, good, obedient to their own husbands, that the word of God be not blasphemed.*

The question arises should wives be questioned like deacons? The answer is what does

DEACONS AND THEIR WIVES

the Bible say? It says "Even so "... or let these first be proved. I personally have known only one church which questioned wives as well as husbands. For some reason some churches have ignored the fact that deacons and their wives are in a relationship ordained by God, and that choosing a deacon means you are also choosing a deacon's wife. Of course wives are not questioned like a deacon. Their responsibilities sometimes are similar to a deacon and sometimes they are entirely different. Their dedication to God and their husband's duties as a deacon should be established. A few questions that could be asked are:

1. Tell us about your salvation experience.
2. Tell us what duties and responsibilities you are now performing for your church and God.
3. Are you pleased your husband is being considered to serve as a deacon?
4. Are you willing to support him in performing the duties and responsibilities as a deacon?
5. Have you read the church Covenant, Statement of Faith, and Bylaws?
6. Do you have any disagreement with these documents? If so elaborate.
7. Do you know of any problems which could prevent your husband from being a faithful servant as a deacon? If so elaborate.
8. Have you read and studied the Biblical commandments detailed in the scripture concerning serving as a deacon and a deacon's wife?

9. Are you aware of anything that should prevent you from serving as a deacon's wife? If so elaborate.

Even though women are forbidden to usurp authority over a man they were included in meetings for prayer with the apostles.

Today women play a very important part in the numerous tasks they perform in serving the Lord. The Bible gives us many examples of women who were very obedient in serving our Lord. Consider Phebe a servant in the church at Cenchrea. She was a "succourer" or helper in time of need. Consider Mary the mother of Jesus. Consider Tabitha, a woman full of good works, charity, and deeds of mercy. Consider Lydia whose heart the Lord opened. She attended or paid attention to what Paul was teaching. Consider Damaris who clung to Paul. Consider the numerous others such as Sarah, Rahab, Ruth, Esther, Mary and numerous others.

> **Acts 1:14** *These all continued with one accord in prayer and supplication, with the women, and Mary the mother of Jesus, and with his brethren.*
>
> **Romans 16:1-2** *I commend unto you Phebe our sister, which is a servant of the church which is at Cenchrea: That ye receive her in the Lord, as becometh saints, and that ye assist her in whatsoever business she hath need of*

you: for she hath been a succourer of many, and of myself also.

Acts 9:36 *Now there was at Joppa a certain disciple named Tabitha, which by interpretation is called Dorcas: this woman was full of good works and almsdeeds which she did.*

Acts 16:14-15 *And a certain woman named Lydia, a seller of purple, of the city of Thyatira, which worshipped God, heard us: whose heart the Lord opened, that she attended unto the things which were spoken of Paul. And when she was baptized, and her household, she besought us, saying, If ye have judged me to be faithful to the Lord, come into my house, and abide there. And she constrained us.*

Women also stood by Jesus even at the latter part of his crucifixion. I suspect many men and women flew the coop when the three hour darkness occurred, the temple vail was torn, the earth quaked, and many saints came out of their graves and were seen by many. That should put the fear of God in everyone, especially unbelievers. When Joseph the counselor and Nicodemus a priest placed Jesus in the tomb it was women who followed them to observe how the body was laid.

Matthew 27:45 *Now from the sixth hour there was darkness over all the land unto the ninth hour.*

***Matthew 27:51-53** And, behold, the veil of the temple was rent in twain from the top to the bottom; and the earth did quake, and the rocks rent; And the graves were opened; and many bodies of the saints which slept arose, And came out of the graves after his resurrection, and went into the holy city, and appeared unto many.*

***Matthew 27:55** And many women were there beholding afar off, which followed Jesus from Galilee, ministering unto him:*

***Luke 23:55** And the women also, which came with him from Galilee, followed after, and beheld the sepulchre, and how his body was laid.*

Women, whether or not they are pastors' or deacons' wives, have and will always be prominent servants to our Lord and Savior Jesus Christ.

CHURCH APPROVAL

After all questioning of candidates and their wives, the deacon board should meet again for discussion. If the candidate is approved the <u>pastor</u> should present his name with a statement as to his and her qualifications to the church. The church should vote their approval. The candidate and his family should not be present when the vote is taken. Should there be an objection, the pastor should meet with the objector in private to

DEACONS AND THEIR WIVES

determine the truth of the matter. The pastor makes the final judgment. If it is a no go, the candidate should withdraw his name from further consideration. Otherwise, the vote should be retaken after the explanation by the pastor. The pastor must have the final say.

FINDING NEW CANDIDATES

It should be noted that a perfect candidate for a deacon will never be found. They should <u>never</u> be chosen because that's all you have. If a candidate is difficult to find it may be necessary for the pastor to teach classes on Biblical requirements for deacons in order to motivate men to seek this position and prove their ability as a servant. Since all church members would have the final vote on approval they too need to be taught appropriate things as well as the men.

> **Psalm 86:11** *Teach me thy way, O LORD; I will walk in thy truth: unite my heart to fear thy name.*
>
> **Psalm 119:33-34** *HE. Teach me, O LORD, the way of thy statutes; and I shall keep it unto the end. Give me understanding, and I shall keep thy law; yea, I shall observe it with my whole heart.*
>
> **Proverbs 9:9** *Give instruction to a wise man, and he will be yet wiser: teach a just man, and he will increase in learning.*

> **Acts 5:42** *And daily in the temple, and in every house, they ceased not to teach and preach Jesus Christ.*
>
> **Ephesians 4:11-12** *And he gave some, apostles; and some, prophets; and some, evangelists; and some, pastors and teachers; For the perfecting of the saints, for the work of the ministry, for the edifying of the body of Christ:*

UNDERSTANDING

Deacons must understand their role in support of the pastor. He alone delegates certain tasks which he expects them to accomplish. These responsibilities should further the growth of the church and are in addition to the commands required in the Bible for every Christian. The important thing is they must recognize their responsibilities as a servant and be one. Pastors should have meetings with the deacons to assure duties are designated and to hold deacons accountable. Also, and most important, determine their walk with God. There must be a clear understanding between a pastor and his deacons. To misunderstand what the pastor expects leads to problems. Deacons will hold back even of informing their pastor of the mood or problems of the members. Some deacons will just sit and wait. Others may lean too far out of the saddle. These things will hinder church growth and could cause problems in the church

John 12:26 *If any man serve me, let him follow me; and where I am, there shall also my servant be: if any man serve me, him will my Father honour.*

Ephesians 6:5-7 *Servants, be obedient to them that are your masters according to the flesh, with fear and trembling, in singleness of your heart, as unto Christ; Not with eyeservice, as menpleasers; but as the servants of Christ, doing the will of God from the heart; With good will doing service, as to the Lord, and not to men:*

PASTORS NEEDS

Pastors also have needs. Such things as church problems, family, home, income, health needs, transportation, etc. Overwhelming administrative problems can grow like a cancer if they are not solved. Pastors also need special times to relax.

They may not want everyone to know their problems. At least **one** deacon should have the responsibility to help the pastor and his family if required. Deacons should encourage the pastor and on special occasions recognize him and his family before the church. Pastors cannot be available twenty four a day, seven days a week to pastor his flock. As a church grows deacons should help with the increasing workload. Deacons could, if assigned by the pastor, be the first point of contact to support church members' problems. Larger problems would be referred to the pastor. This arrangement can save the pastor considerable time which he could use more effectively on prayer, study, ministering, church business, and even more quality time with his family and friends. Pastors are not robots. They need encouragement, understanding, and support.

TRUST

Deacons and pastors must have complete trust in working together. Their business must be strictly confidential with <u>NO</u> <u>leaks</u>. Pastors alone inform the church NOT deacons. When pastors meet with deacons on church business there must be honest discussions, but when they leave the meeting deacons must put 100% support and agreement with the pastor's conclusion. Deacons who disclose what goes on at these meetings with church members, including their wives, contrary to the pastor's direction are busy bodies when they should be peace makers. Any such deacon has violated their office as a deacon and should be counseled by the pastor to maintain unity and growth in the church.

> ***2 Thessalonians 3:11*** *For we hear that there are some which walk among you disorderly, working not at all, but are busybodies.*

> ***1 Peter 4:15*** *But let none of you suffer as a murderer, or as a thief, or as an*

evildoer, or as a busybody in other men's matters.

DEACONS OFFICES

As far as I understand there is no Biblical requirement for offices within the deacons. However, such offices could be most helpful for the success of deacons' support of the pastor and growth of the church. Also it gives the pastor more control over his deacons in fulfilling their assigned responsibilities. For example, a chairman may be assigned to look after the needs of the pastor and his family among other duties at the desire of the pastor. A secretary could be assigned to keep the minutes of all meetings and to read the minutes of the last meeting and report on accomplishments or the lack thereof. Deacons could hold an office to be responsible for distributing flowers or fruit baskets, visiting the sick, and performing benevolence responsibilities. Many other tasks could be and should be assigned by the pastor. <u>All</u> deacons must always demonstrate their faithfulness in appointed and Biblical duties such as soulwinning, teaching, and caring for the needy. Remember as the church grows so does the need to increase the number of deacons.

2 Timothy 2:15 *Study to shew thyself approved unto God, a workman that needeth not to be ashamed, rightly dividing the word of truth.*

ROTATION

Many churches rotate deacons in and out of serving as a deacon. They say it gives all the men a chance to serve as if it is not everyone's responsibility to serve <u>whether</u> <u>or</u> <u>not</u> they are a deacon. This is not taught in the Bible no more than rotating a pastor in and out of his position as the pastor of a church. I believe when everyone works to build a church more deacons could and should be added. Also, deacons move, get old and die off. Therefore, normal attrition will give others an opportunity to be deacons. No one should sit back and do nothing because they do not have the title of a deacon. If they won't serve the Lord before, they won't serve even if they were a deacon.

Romans 11:29 *For the gifts and calling of God are without repentance.*

2 Timothy 4:2 *Preach the word; be instant in season, out of season; reprove, rebuke, exhort with all longsuffering and doctrine.*

HIGH WATER MARK

Stephen and Philip set the high water mark for all deacons. They were among the first seven chosen by the people. They served and most importantly the work of God increased.

Acts 6:5 And the saying pleased the whole multitude: and they chose Stephen, a man full of faith and of the Holy Ghost, and Philip, and Prochorus, and Nicanor, and Timon, and Parmenas, and Nicolas a proselyte of Antioch:

Acts 6:7 And the word of God increased; and the number of the disciples multiplied in Jerusalem greatly; and a great company of the priests were obedient to the faith.

DEACON STEPHEN

Stephen was full of faith and power. He performed great wonders and miracles among the people. No one could resist his wisdom and the spirit by which he spoke. He was accused of blasphemy but that did not stop him from teaching and preaching Jesus. He was finally brought before the council. While he was being accused his face was seen as if it was the face of an angel. He didn't run. He stood and preached. After which his accusers were cut to the heart and took him out and stoned him to death. His last words were for God to forgive his executioners. Stephen taught, preached, and gave his life the cause of Christ. He apparently had a great influence on Paul who participated in the stoning. Stephen was the first New Testament martyr to wear the martyr's crown. One might say that was then, this is now. In other words, we give up with half-hearted or no service.

There is absolutely no reason deacons and others could not demonstrate a like commitment.

> ***Acts 6:8** And Stephen, full of faith and power, did great wonders and miracles among the people.*
>
> ***Acts 6:10-12** And they were not able to resist the wisdom and the spirit by which he spake. Then they suborned men, which said, We have heard him speak blasphemous words against Moses, and against God. And they stirred up the people, and the elders, and the scribes, and came upon him, and caught him, and brought him to the council,*
>
> ***Acts 6:15** And all that sat in the council, looking stedfastly on him, saw his face as it had been the face of an angel.*
>
> ***Acts 7:54-60** When they heard these things, they were cut to the heart, and they gnashed on him with their teeth. But he, being full of the Holy Ghost, looked up stedfastly into heaven, and saw the glory of God, and Jesus standing on the right hand of God, And said, Behold, I see the heavens opened, and the Son of man standing on the right hand of God. Then they cried out with a loud voice, and stopped their ears, and ran upon him with one*

accord, And cast him out of the city, and stoned him: and the witnesses laid down their clothes at a young man's feet, whose name was Saul. And they stoned Stephen, calling upon God, and saying, Lord Jesus, receive my spirit. And he kneeled down, and cried with a loud voice, Lord, lay not this sin to their charge. And when he had said this, he fell asleep.

DEACON PHILIP

Philip, one of the seven, was another deacon totally sold out to Christ. He, like Stephen, taught and preached the Word of God. He was engaged in a revival when an angel told him to go to Gaza, a desert. He did not argue or wait until after this revival. Without any more information of why, he unconditionally obeyed God and went. You know the story of the eunuch of how he was saved and baptized. We can assume that this eunuch took the gospel back to Ethiopia. Philip apparently introduced the gospel through the eunuch to north Africa. Another great truth that God allowed Philip to testify to is recorded in Chapter 8 of the book of Acts. After the eunuch was saved he asked Philip a very direct question, "What doth hinder me to be baptized?" Philip answered saying, "If thou believeth with all thine heart, thou mayest." What hinders new Christians to be baptized? Only believing! Nothing should be added to or taken away from God's commanded instructions. Philip had great success as an evangelical preacher.

Acts 8:5 Then Philip went down to the city of Samaria, and preached Christ unto them.

Acts 8:26 And the angel of the Lord spake unto Philip, saying, Arise, and go toward the south unto the way that goeth down from Jerusalem unto Gaza, which is desert.

Acts 8:35-38 Then Philip opened his mouth, and began at the same scripture, and preached unto him Jesus. And as they went on their way, they came unto a certain water: and the eunuch said, See, here is water; what doth hinder me to be baptized? And Philip said, If thou believest with all thine heart, thou mayest. And he answered and said, I believe that Jesus Christ is the Son of God. And he commanded the chariot to stand still: and they went down both into the water, both Philip and the eunuch; and he baptized him.

INSPIRATION

These two deacons should inspire all of us. They not only served as great deacons but God expanded their responsibilities to preaching and baptizing converts. They truly have set the high water mark that all deacons should strive for. They yielded their total being to further the gospel of

Christ. They were <u>great</u> <u>SERVANTS</u> of God. Could deacons today do the work of Stephen or Philip? Of course, <u>if</u> we would totally yield to the will of God and be His servant.

> ***Romans 12:1-2*** *I beseech you therefore, brethren, by the mercies of God, that ye present your bodies a living sacrifice, holy, acceptable unto God, which is your reasonable service. And be not conformed to this world: but be ye transformed by the renewing of your mind, that ye may prove what is that good, and acceptable, and perfect, will of God.*

FOLLOW THE LEADER

Deacons were and are to be proven examples of Christian faith. The primary purpose of a deacon is to be a SERVANT. A servant under the direct authority of the pastor. It would be a mistake for a pastor not to use their wisdom while remembering they are only a SERVANT. Deacons can assist the church in its business and financial responsibilities, but they are only a SERVANT. To be effective they <u>must</u> meet Biblical requirements and have <u>proven</u> ability to perform in that position <u>before</u> they are even considered for this God ordained position.

> ***John 15:16*** *Ye have not chosen me, but I have chosen you, and ordained you, that ye should go and bring forth fruit, and that your fruit should remain:*

that whatsoever ye shall ask of the Father in my name, he may give it you.

OTHER DUTIES

Since deacons should have proven abilities they would already be performing tasks in support of the ministry. One may ask what <u>additional</u> duties were appointed to the first seven deacons. The Bible doesn't say probably because as a church grows so does the workload and new tasks that need to be performed. Also, some deacons could probably think their only requirement is to serve "tables", meaning in today's environment only participate in serving the Lord's Supper. It is up to pastors in today's church to establish the responsibilities of a deacon and last, but not least, **<u>hold them responsible and accountable</u>**. A deacon should never be overwhelmed with his responsibilities. The church should ordain more <u>faithful</u> and <u>proven</u> men as deacons as the workload grows. Ordaining deacons is a very serious responsibility of a church. Too many times deacons are chosen for their popularity and <u>not</u> their service. When this happens the requirements for performing all tasks fall right back onto the pastor's lap, and many will be left undone. It would be very difficult for the church to grow if the deacons don't "deke". One must remember that Jesus said of lukewarm churches, he could spew them out of his mouth. What about lukewarm deacons?

***Colossians 1:9-10** For this cause we also, since the day we heard it, do not* *cease to pray for you, and to desire that ye might be filled with the knowledge of his will in all wisdom and spiritual understanding; That ye might walk worthy of the Lord unto all pleasing, being fruitful in every good work, and increasing in the knowledge of God;*

Revelation 3:14-16 *And unto the angel of the church of the Laodiceans write; These things saith the Amen, the faithful and true witness, the beginning of the creation of God; I know thy works, that thou art neither cold nor hot: I would thou wert cold or hot. So then because thou art lukewarm, and neither cold nor hot, I will spue thee out of my mouth.*

NEGLECTED DUTIES

Some deacons do not even attend church regularly. Many do not pass out tracts, visit the sick, knock on doors, and rarely, if ever, attempt to tell anyone about Christ. Many will faithfully give their money to God but not their time. They are perfectly content in being a deacon in name only.

Hebrews 10:25 *Not forsaking the assembling of ourselves together, as the manner of some is; but exhorting one another: and so much the more, as ye see the day approaching.*

> ***Mark 16:15** And he said unto them, Go ye into all the world, and preach the gospel to every creature.*

They do not consider that God will hold all deacons accountable just like he will hold pastors and saints accountable. They sometimes forget they are in a leadership position as deacons set apart for one purpose, that is to be a servant in helping to grow the ministry of the church.

> ***2 Corinthians 5:10** For we must all appear before the judgment seat of Christ; that every one may receive the things done in his body, according to that he hath done, whether it be good or bad.*

> ***1 Corinthians 3:13-15** Every man's work shall be made manifest: for the day shall declare it, because it shall be revealed by fire; and the fire shall try every man's work of what sort it is. If any man's work abide which he hath built thereupon, he shall receive a reward. If any man's work shall be burned, he shall suffer loss: but he himself shall be saved; yet so as by fire.*

> ***1 John 2:28** And now, little children, abide in him; that, when he shall appear, we may have confidence, and not be ashamed before him at his coming.*

> ***John 14:21*** *He that hath my commandments, and keepeth them, he it is that loveth me: and he that loveth me shall be loved of my Father, and I will love him, and will manifest myself to him.*

DEMONSTRATE FAITH

A good deacon is an example of Christian faith. They demonstrate their faith in all manner of service directed by their pastor and God's Holy Word. It should be remembered that the Bible establishes many, many commandments which all Christians should perform, <u>especially</u> deacons. These should be performed automatically by deacons without having to be reminded of by the pastor.

> ***Hebrews 11:6*** *But without faith it is impossible to please him: for he that cometh to God must believe that he is, and that he is a rewarder of them that diligently seek him.*

> ***John 14:21*** *He that hath my commandments, and keepeth them, he it is that loveth me: and he that loveth me shall be loved of my Father, and I will love him, and will manifest myself to him.*

> ***1 John 2:3-4*** *And hereby we do know that we know him, if we keep his commandments. He that saith, I know*

him, and keepeth not his commandments, is a liar, and the truth is not in him.

John 15:10 *If ye keep my commandments, ye shall abide in my love; even as I have kept my Father's commandments, and abide in his love.*

PASTOR/DEACONS MEETINGS

Pastors must meet with their deacons often to assure a meeting of minds, training, instructing, advising, assigning tasks, and assuring accountability. Without meetings deacons' support will rarely occur. Pastors should call for such meetings often and as the need arise, but not less than monthly is not too often.

Deacons must be faithful to all tasks assigned. They should never not perform a task or perform it a time or two and quit. They must also continually demonstrate they are living up to Biblical standards to the very best of their ability and they should avoid a worldly lifestyle.

Romans 10:17 *So then faith cometh by hearing, and hearing by the word of God.*

James 2:20 *But wilt thou know, O vain man, that faith without works is dead?*

Hebrews 11:6 *But without faith it is impossible to please him: for he that* *cometh to God must believe that he is, and that he is a rewarder of them that diligently seek him.*

Pastors must be in charge of all deacon meetings unless he specifically allows a deacons meeting for a special purpose which does not merit his presence. In such cases the Chairman of the deacons presides and he must report back to the pastor. (If for some reason the pastor is being disciplined Church Bylaws should be followed.) A meeting may be requested by a deacon to the pastor for his consideration, but the final decision remains with the pastor. Before a meeting is adjourned the pastor should give his final conclusion. All deacons should leave the meeting fully supporting his conclusion even though <u>in the meeting</u> they may have offered conflicting opinions. In all case meetings are strictly confidential unless understood differently from the pastor, that means don't tell your wives as well as others. Spreading information from meetings always leads to gossip and distortion from the truth. Pastors are responsible for informing the church, not deacons. Deacons should not be a busy body involving themselves in the affairs and responsibilities of the pastor. I have been in meetings where by the time I got home my wife was receiving phone calls of confidential information which was totally wrong. These leaks caused unnecessary problems which were not easily corrected.

***1 Peter 4:15** But let none of you suffer as a murderer, or as a thief, or as an* *evildoer, or as a busybody in other men's matters.*

STAND

Our pastor, Nathan Nix, recently preached a great message on "Standing" by putting on the whole armor of God. Paul said be "strong in the Lord, and the power of his might." To stand against our enemy the devil we must be protected by God's armor. God's armor is "truth, righteousness, the gospel of peace," above all "faith, salvation, and the word of God." He said pray always. That's armor, God's armor. We can stand against the wicked. Paul said "….having done all, to stand." Deacons should be prepared and STAND.

> ***Ephesians 6:10-19*** *Finally, my brethren, be strong in the Lord, and in the power of his might. Put on the whole armour of God, that ye may be able to stand against the wiles of the devil. For we wrestle not against flesh and blood, but against principalities, against powers, against the rulers of the darkness of this world, against spiritual wickedness in high places. Wherefore take unto you the whole armour of God, that ye may be able to withstand in the evil day, and having done all, to stand. Stand therefore, having your loins girt about with truth, and having on the breastplate of righteousness; And your feet shod with*

the preparation of the gospel of peace; Above all, taking the shield of faith, wherewith ye shall be able to quench all the fiery darts of the wicked. And take the helmet of salvation, and the sword of the Spirit, which is the word of God: Praying always with all prayer and supplication in the Spirit, and watching thereunto with all perseverance and supplication for all saints; And for me, that utterance may be given unto me, that I may open my mouth boldly, to make known the mystery of the gospel,

Colossians 3:17 *And whatsoever ye do in word or deed, do all in the name of the Lord Jesus, giving thanks to God and the Father by him.*

Colossians 4:6 *Let your speech be alway with grace, seasoned with salt, that ye may know how ye ought to answer every man.*

Galatians 5:1 *Stand fast therefore in the liberty wherewith Christ hath made us free, and be not entangled again with the yoke of bondage.*

1 Thessalonians 3:8 *For now we live, if ye stand fast in the Lord.*

CONCLUSION

I have not meant to be discouraging for men seeking or holding the office of a deacon. I only mean to present what I've learned from the Bible and fifty plus years in serving as a deacon. I believe all Christians should be striving to perform the same tasks as deacons. I believe deacons first prove themselves as perhaps being more mature than some who have had less knowledge and experience. I believe deacons are chosen and ordained to serve the people as a mature servant under the leadership of the pastor. These responsibilities are in the direct support of the numerous tasks required to grow a church. They are most importantly designed to relieve the pastor of menial tasks which would hinder his ability to perform his pastoral responsibilities. Serving as a good deacon offers great rewards in this life and all eternity. If you seek the office of a deacon you seek a good thing!

> ***Luke 11:9-10*** *And I say unto you, Ask, and it shall be given you; seek, and ye shall find; knock, and it shall be opened unto you. For every one that asketh receiveth; and he that seeketh findeth; and to him that knocketh it shall be opened.*
>
> ***Mark 8:34*** *And when he had called the people unto him with his disciples also, he said unto them, Whosoever will*

come after me, let him deny himself, and take up his cross, and follow me.

***Luke 6:46** And why call ye me, Lord, Lord, and do not the things which I say?*

***Colossians 1:10** That ye might walk worthy of the Lord unto all pleasing, being fruitful in every good work, and increasing in the knowledge of God;*

***Colossians 3:23** And whatsoever ye do, do it heartily, as to the Lord, and not unto men;*

***Galatians 6:9** And let us not be weary in well doing: for in due season we shall reap, if we faint not.*

SALVATION

If you have read this book and are not 100% sure you have a free ticket to heaven paid for by the precious blood of Jesus Christ read on to see what the Bible says.

The Bible teaches us that we are all sinners and deserve to die and be cast into hell to be tormented day and night for all eternity. It also teaches us that God loved us and provided the only way to be cleansed from our sins. That is to repent of our sins, trust Jesus in redeeming our souls through the shedding of His precious Blood on the Cross of Calvary. Trust Jesus and be saved today.

Romans 5:12 *Wherefore, as by one man sin entered into the world, and death by sin; and so death passed upon all men, for that all have sinned:*

Romans 3:23 *For all have sinned, and come short of the glory of God;*

Romans 6:23 *For the wages of sin is death; but the gift of God is eternal life through Jesus Christ our Lord.*

Luke 16:23 *And in hell he lift up his eyes, being in torments, and seeth Abraham afar off, and Lazarus in his bosom.*

John 3:16 *For God so loved the world, that he gave his only begotten Son, that whosoever believeth in him should not perish, but have everlasting life.*

John 3:36 *He that believeth on the Son hath everlasting life: and he that believeth not the Son shall not see life; but the wrath of God abideth on him.*

Romans 5:8 *But God commendeth his love toward us, in that, while we were yet sinners, Christ died for us.*

Revelation 20:14 *And death and hell were cast into the lake of fire. This is the second death.*

DEACONS AND THEIR WIVES

Mark 1:15 *And saying, The time is fulfilled, and the kingdom of God is at hand: repent ye, and believe the gospel.*

1 Corinthians 15:3-5 *For I delivered unto you first of all that which I also received, how that Christ died for our sins according to the scriptures; And that he was buried, and that he rose again the third day according to the scriptures: And that he was seen of Cephas, then of the twelve:*

1 John 1:7 *But if we walk in the light, as he is in the light, we have fellowship one with another, and the blood of Jesus Christ his Son cleanseth us from all sin.*

2 Corinthians 5:21 *For he hath made him to be sin for us, who knew no sin; that we might be made the righteousness of God in him.*

Romans 10:13 *For whosoever shall call upon the name of the Lord shall be saved.*

Acts 10:43 *To him give all the prophets witness, that through his name whosoever believeth in him shall receive remission of sins.*

1 John 5:10-13 *He that believeth on the Son of God hath the witness in himself: he that believeth not God hath made him a liar; because he believeth not the record that God gave of his Son. And this is the record, that God hath given to us eternal life, and this life is in his Son. He that hath the Son hath life; and he that hath not the Son of God hath not life. These things have I written unto you that believe on the name of the Son of God; that ye may know that ye have eternal life, and that ye may believe on the name of the Son of God.*

John 10:28 *And I give unto them eternal life; and they shall never perish, neither shall any man pluck them out of my hand.*

INDEX

abilities, 12, 58
all nations, 15, 19
apostles, 13, 16, 21, 25, 27, 29, 36, 44, 48
arose, 26, 46
assist, 3, 7, 11, 14, 21, 27, 40, 45, 58
assisting, 10
attempting, 12, 35
attendant, 10
authority, 3, 11, 36, 44, 58
baptized, 14, 15, 17, 46, 56, 57
believers, 14, 28, 38
Bible, 2, 4, 10, 11, 22, 25, 33, 36, 37, 40-44 49, 52, 58, 61, 66, 68
Bill Penell, 32
bishops, 12
blind, 15
body of Christ, 11, 13, 21, 29, 49
book, 3-5, 10, 12, 23, 56, 68
building, 11, 15, 28
chain, 15, 16, 18
chosen, 6, 10, 24, 25, 28, 32, 48, 53, 58, 59, 66
Christians, 12, 22, 25, 39, 40, 56, 62, 66
church, 3, 4, 5, 7, 10, 11, 13, 15, 18, 21, 25, 27-29, 31, 32, 34, 36-39, 41, 42,-45, 47-53, 58, 59-60, 64, 66
churches, 4, 7, 10, 25, 39, 43, 52, 59
commanded, 12, 15, 17, 39, 56, 57
commandments, 15, 25, 26, 29, 44, 61, 62
compel, 16
continue, 10, 15, 26
continued, 15, 45
converts, 7, 57
creature, 15, 16, 60
culling, 15
Curtis Hutson, 12
deacon, 5-7, 10, 11, 16, 29, 31-35, 37, 40-44, 47, 50-52, 56, 58-61, 63, 66
DEACONS, 1, 8, 9, 13, 27, 28, 30, 32, 36, 37, 40, 51, 62
defined, 10
demonstrated, 10, 35, 42

INDEX OF WORDS AND PHRASES

desires, 11, 31, 33
disciples, 13, 15, 16, 23-26, 53, 67
Don Richards, 12
duties, 3, 10, 28, 31, 32, 35, 36, 41, 42, 44, 49, 52, 58
every house, 13, 14, 48
example, 12, 20, 21, 22, 41, 52, 61
expect, 12, 28, 32
experience, 10, 37, 44, 66
experiences, 7
failures, 12
faith, 6, 13, 15, 16, 18, 22, 26, 27, 35, 39, 53, 54, 58, 61-65
feast, 15
fifty plus years, 7, 11, 66
filled, 13, 16-18, 39, 40, 59
five thousand, 13, 14
goal, 10
God, 3, 6, 7, 11-14, 17-23, 25-27, 29-35, 37-40, 42-46, 49, 50, 52-70
gospel, 15, 16, 18, 32, 56, 57, 60, 64, 65, 69

great pastors, 12
grounded, 15
group, 3
grow, 10, 13, 25, 50, 59, 60, 66
growing, 7
hedges, 15
help, 3, 12, 13, 16, 20, 25, 28, 29, 41, 50
highways, 15
Holy Word, 7, 12, 61
honor, 11
host, 10
house, 16, 24, 34, 35, 39, 41, 46
importance, 15
improve, 12
Jerusalem, 13, 16, 17, 19, 27, 38, 53, 56
Jesus, 7, 11-22, 26, 30, 35, 36, 38, 39, 45-48, 54, 55, 57, 59, 66, 68, 70
Jesus Christ, 12, 13, 14, 17, 20, 35, 38, 39, 47, 48, 57, 68, 70
John, 11, 12, 16, 17, 22-24, 26, 49, 58, 61, 62, 69, 70, 71
judge, 15
KJV, 11

73

knowledge, 10, 13, 19, 22, 59, 66, 67
learned, 11, 66
Luke, 11, 12, 15, 19, 30, 47, 67, 68
maimed, 15
members, 3, 10, 18, 21, 28, 39, 48, 49, 50, 51
menial, 10, 25, 28, 29, 67
minister, 10, 14, 25
ministering, 13, 47, 50
murmur, 13
neglected, 13, 25, 27, 29
New Testament Church, 13, 25
Nix, Nathan, 65, 85
office, 3, 7, 10, 12, 16, 29, 33, 35, 40, 51, 52, 66
ordain, 13, 59
overwhelmed, 10, 59
parable, 15
pastors, 6, 10, 12, 13, 20, 21, 28, 29, 31, 32, 47, 48, 51, 59, 60
Paul, 12, 17, 33, 41, 45, 46, 54, 64
people, 3, 10, 13, 15, 17, 20, 22, 25, 33, 35-38, 40, 53, 54, 66, 67
perfection, 7, 10
Peter, 12, 51, 64
Philip, 12, 27, 53, 56, 57
Philippians, 12, 18
poor, 15
position, 10, 13, 29, 48, 52, 58, 60
power, 15-17, 28, 29, 31, 32, 54, 64, 65
preach, 14-17, 28, 48, 60
preached, 13, 19, 20, 54, 56, 64
problem, 13
proved, 12, 16, 25, 35, 40, 41, 43
purpose, 3, 10, 11, 15, 21, 25, 32, 38, 58, 60, 63
qualifications, 7, 17, 33, 40, 41, 47
received, 14, 16, 18, 69
required, 10, 28, 38, 43, 49, 50, 66
requirement, 25, 51, 59
responsibilities, 3, 6, 7, 10, 12, 31, 32, 41, 43, 44, 49, 52, 57, 58, 59, 64, 66

INDEX OF WORDS AND PHRASES

run errands, 10
saved, 13, 15, 17, 20, 56, 61, 68, 70
saving, 7, 38
seek, 3, 10, 31, 48, 62, 63, 67
Servants, 49
SERVANTS, 7, 8, 25, 27, 57
serve, 10, 11, 13, 20, 25, 27, 31, 37, 42, 44, 49, 52, 59, 66
Shoot for the moon, 12
souls, 7, 14, 22, 68
Stephen, 12, 27, 53-57
striving, 12, 18, 66
tasks, 10, 25, 28, 29, 43, 44, 49, 52, 58, 63, 66
taught, 13, 15, 20, 48, 52, 54, 56
teach, 14, 15, 16, 28, 32, 33, 43, 48
teacher, 10
teaches, 7, 33, 68
three thousand, 13, 14
together, 5, 13, 17, 18, 37, 51, 60

tomb, 15, 38, 46
try, 12, 61
unbroken, 15, 16, 18
understanding, 10, 19, 41, 48-50, 59
unending, 15, 16, 18
unworthy, 15
uttermost, 17
William Pennell, 12
wisely, 10
witness, 17, 18, 26, 39, 59, 70
wives, 10, 32, 35, 41, 43, 47, 51, 64
word, 10, 14, 15, 20, 21, 23, 26, 27, 30, 32, 35, 37, 43, 52, 53, 63-66
Word of God, 7, 56
words, 10, 23, 24, 30, 54
work, 12-14, 21, 26, 28, 29, 45, 46, 48, 60, 65
workload, 10, 50, 58
world, 15, 16, 19, 22, 24, 35, 57, 60, 65, 68, 69
written, 10, 11, 19, 25, 33, 37, 70

SCRIPTURE REFERENCES

BOOK	PAGE
PSALMS 86:11	48
PSALMS 119:33-34	48
PROVERBS: 1:7	19
PROVERBS 9:9	48
PROVERBS 20:1	35
PROVERBS 27:17	5
PROVERBS 29:18	33
ECCLESIASTES 7:20	33
HABAKKUK 2:15	35
MATTHEW 5:13-16	24
MATTHEW 6:24	11
MATTHEW 27:45	46
MATTHEW 27:51-53	47
MATTHEW 27:55	47
MATTHEW 28:18-20	15
MARK 1:15	70
MARK 8:34	67
MARK 9:41	21

SCRIPTURE REFERENCES

MARK 16:15	16, 61
LUKE 4:8	11
LUKE 6:46	68
LUKE 9:23	12, 19
LUKE 9:26	30
LUKE 10:2	15
LUKE 11:9-10	67
LUKE 16:23	69
LUKE 23:55	47
LUKE 24:45-47	19
JOHN 3:16	69
JOHN 3:36	69
JOHN 5:24	26
JOHN 8:31	26
JOHN 10:28	71
JOHN 12:26	50
JOHN 14:21	62
JOHN 15:1-8	23
JOHN 15:10	63
JOHN 15:16	24, 58

JOHN 12:26	11
ACTS 1:4-5	17
ACTS l:8-9	17
ACTS 1:14	45
ACTS 2:4	14, 18
ACTS 4:4	14
ACTS 4:10-12	20
ACTS 5:42	14, 49
ACTS 6:1-7	27
ACTS 6:3	31, 40
ACTS 6:5	54
ACTS 6:8	55
ACTS 7:54-60	55, 56
ACTS 8:5	56
ACTS 8:26	57
ACTS 8:35-38	57
ACTS 9:36	46
ACTS 10:43	70
ACTS 16:14-15	46
ROMANS 1:14	18

SCRIPTURE REFERENCES

ROMANS 1:16	32
ROMANS 2:5-6	19
ROMANS 3:10	33
ROMANS 5:12	69
ROMANS 9:23	30
ROMANS 10:17	63
ROMANS 3:23	33, 69
ROMANS 5:8	69
ROMANS 6:23	69
ROMANS 10:17	26, 63
ROMANS 11:29	53
ROMANS 10:13	70
ROMANS 12:1	7
ROMANS 12:1-2	58
ROMANS 16:1-2	45
1 CORINTHIANS 3:7, 8	23
1 CORINTHIANS 3:13-15	61
1 CORINTHIANS 15:3-5	70
1 CORINTHIANS 15:58	30
2 CORINTHIANS 5:10	61

2 CORINTHIANS 5:21	70
GALATIANS 5:1	66
GALATIANS 6:9	68
EPHESIANS 1:19	17
EPHESIANS 2:10	7, 21
EPHESIANS 4:11-12	29, 49
EPHESIANS 4:11-13	21
EPHESIANS 4:30	21
EPHESIANS 5:1	29
EPHESIANS 6:5-7	50
EPHESIANS 6:10	28
EPHESIANS 6:10-19	65
PHILIPPIANS 1:1	12
PHILIPPIANS 1:27	18
COLOSSIANS 1:9-10	59
COLOSSIANS 1:10	68
COLOSSIANS 3:17	66
COLOSSIANS 3:23	68
COLOSSIANS 4:6	66
1 THESSALONIANS 3:8	66

SCRIPTURE REFERENCES

2 THESSALONIANS 3:11	51
1 TIMOTHY 1:15	19
1 TIMOTHY 3:1-8	34
1 TIMOTHY 3:8-13	35
1 TIMOTHY 3:8	42
1 TIMOTHY 3:10	16, 40
1 TIMOTHY 3:11	41
2 TIMOTHY 2:15	30, 32, 52
2 TIMOTHY 4:2	53
TITUS 2:1	43
TITUS 2:3	43
TITUS 2:3-5	43
HEBREWS 6:9-10	14
HEBREWS 9:14	11
HEBREWS 10:25	60
HEBREWS 11:6	62, 63
JAMES 1:22	21
JAMES 2:10	33
JAMES 2:20	22, 63
1 PETER 4:15	51, 64

1 JOHN 1:7	70
1 JOHN 2:3-4	62
1 JOHN 2:4	26
1 JOHN 2:6	16
1 JOHN 2:28	61
1 JOHN 5:10	26
1 JOHN 5:10-13	71
REVELATION 3:14-16	60
REVELATION 14:12	26
REVELATION 20:14	69

ABOUT THE AUTHOR

LEO & ELSIE LAVINKA

LEO ROBERT LAVINKA WAS BORN IN 1934. HE WAS RAISED IN MONTICELLO, FLORIDA, BUT NOT IN A CHRISTIAN HOME. AFTER HIGH SCHOOL AND ONE TOUR IN THE AIR FORCE, HE ATTENDED FLORIDA STATE UNIVERSITY BEFORE TRANSFERRING TO THE UNIVERSITY OF FLORIDA WHERE HE GRADUATED WITH A BACHELOR OF CIVIL ENGINEERING DEGREE. HE WORKED FOR THE U.S. ARMY CORPS OF ENGINEERS IN THE

JACKSONVILLE, FLORIDA, DISTRICT BEFORE TRANSFERRING TO THE DIVISION OFFICE IN ATLANTA, GEORGIA IN 1969. HE BEGAN HIS CAREER IN CONSTRUCTION AND HAD OPPORTUNITY TO PARTICIPATE IN MANY DIFFERENT MILITARY AND CIVIL ENGINEERING PROJECTS IN THE SOUTHEAST UNITED STATES, PUERTO RICO, U.S. VIRGIN ISLANDS, PANAMA CANAL ZONE, AND SOMETIMES IN OTHER CENTRAL AND SOUTH AMERICA COUNTRIES.

IN 1973 HE TRANSFERRED FROM CONSTRUCTION TO EMERGENCY MANAGEMENT WHERE HE WAS RESPONSIBLE FOR PLANNING, COORDINATING, TRAINING, AND EXECUTION OF THE CORPS' MISSIONS TO SUPPORT THE MILITARY, AND NATURAL DISASTERS RECOVERY EFFORTS. HIS RESPONSIBILITY EXPANDED TO THE MIDDLE EAST BEFORE AND DURING DESERT SHIELD, DESERT STORM, AND KUWAIT RECOVERY. HE IS THE RECIPIENT OF SEVERAL AWARDS FOR HIS SERVICE AND RETIRED IN 1999 AFTER 39 YEARS OF SERVICE TO THE U.S. GOVERNMENT.

HE WAS SAVED IN 1969 WHILE ATTENDING FORREST HILLS BAPTIST CHURCH IN DECATUR, GEORGIA, UNDER THE MINISTRY OF DR. CURTIS HUTSON AND THE WITNESSING OF A COWORKER. HE WAS ORDAINED AS A DEACON BY PASTOR HUTSON IN 1970. HE ALSO SERVED AS A DEACON AT CORINTH BAPTIST CHURCH, LOGANVILLE, GEORGIA UNDER PASTOR DON RICHARDS; RETURN BAPTIST CHURCH, CLARKSVILLE, GEORGIA UNDER PASTOR WALTER BURRELL; AND

ABOUT THE AUTHOR

IS CURRENTLY A DEACON, TREASURER, AND SECRETARY AT ZION HILL BAPTIST CHURCH, CLEVELAND, GEORGIA UNDER PASTOR NATHAN NIX, (ALL INDEPENDENT, FUNDAMENTAL BAPTIST CHURCHES).

HE HAS TAUGHT SUNDAY SCHOOL FROM ELEMENTARY TO ADULTS IN SEVERAL CHURCHES AND SERVED IN THE BUS MINISTRY AT FORREST HILLS BAPTIST CHURCH. HE HAS ALSO BEEN A JANITOR, YARD KEEPER, AND A TEACHER AT A SATELLITE CHURCH. HE HAS BEEN ACTIVE IN VISITATION PROGRAMS FROM 1970 TO THE PRESENT.

BROTHER LAVINKA IS THE AUTHOR OF SEVERAL OTHER BOOKS:

1. "ETERNAL SALVATION"
2. "ARE YOU READY?"
3. "ANSWERED PRAYERS"

THEY ARE ALL AVAILABLE ON TOP (THE OLD PATHS PUBLICATIONS) WEBPAGE WITH LINKS TO DISTRIBUTORS' WEBSITES HERE:

http://theoldpathspublications.com/Pages/Authors/LaVinka.htm

Printed in the USA
CPSIA information can be obtained
at www.ICGtesting.com
LVHW021224241124
797471LV00008B/802